A JOURNALING PROCESS:

ALIGNING THE HEART AND BRAIN TO CREATE AUTHENTIC ACTION AND TRANSFORMATION

THE HEART-CENTERED *reflections* OF

____

First Edition

www.hopeactualized.com

Published by Kate Butler Books
www.katebutlerbooks.com

ISBN: 978-1-948927-78-9

Design by Margaret Cogswell
margaretcogswell.com

FROM MY *heart* TO YOURS,

Your heart holds so much beautiful power and potential. When we tap into the hidden wealth of wisdom within the heart and welcome an alignment between the heart and mind, clarity shows up and pathways for authentic change appear.

When we allow our hearts to join forces with our minds, forming an alliance for our higher good, we step into our power. We can begin to move forward with the self-acceptance and love of the heart combined with the strategic processing system of the brain working together to create change.

Start in your heart. Tune in as it communicates with your brain, working with it to form a synchronized, highly efficient and integrated partnership. Ideas and actions that rise from this marriage of your heart and brain are energized and powerful. They originate from a place of pure love and abundance, while also containing your brain's strategic abilities to formulate a plan and get things done.

If we bring our unanswered questions, areas of indecision, or divided thinking into a calm and centered heart, our hearts and brains can collaborate to provide our best solutions. The heart has a way of gently reigning in our brain's thoughts of fear and scarcity, while filtering our decisions through love.

My desire is that as you use this journal, you will feel encouraged, empowered, enlightened, and integrated. My heart is sending you beautiful transformation that moves from heart to brain to change.

A BIT OF *science*

Your heart is always sending messages to your brain They are in constant communication. Research shows that the heart is the most powerful communicator in our body, having an information processing system independent of the brain. Scientists refer to our heart's nervous system as the "heart brain" and 80% of all messages within the body originate from the heart, while 20% come from the brain. 90% of the signals from our hearts are sent to our brains and these messages influence higher brain functioning centers involved in emotional processing, cognition, and perception.

In addition to the communication provided through neural pathways between the heart and brain, our hearts communicate through the most powerful electromagnetic field within our bodies. The heart's magnetic field is about 5000 times more powerful that our brain's, radiating to every cell in our bodies and beyond, being measurable outside the body.

Research shows that we are capable of synchronizing our hearts with our brains. By intentionally introducing and sustaining feelings such as love, appreciation, kindness, or calm, we can bring the rhythms of these two organs together, resulting in an increase in harmony within the body's systems. They have also found a significant reduction in mental chatter, increased intuition, and better cognitive functioning. These "positive" emotions also trigger the release of healthy hormones within our bodies, reducing the effects of stress.

(Search "neurocardiology", "heart brain", or look up The HeartMath Institute for further information).

FROM HEART
TO CHANGE
TO BRAIN

HOW *to*:

FORM A HEART-BRAIN ALLIANCE

Start from your heart: Center your attention on the area of your heart. Imagine filling it with breath and life.

Spend a bit of time there, just focusing in on your heart.

Create a "positive" feeling such as love, kindness, appreciation, peace, or joy. Sometimes it helps to recreate a feeling from a positive past experience. Bring this emotion deeply into your heart.

Maintain that "positive" emotion and send it to your brain.

Invite open communication and alignment between your heart and your brain. Let your heart's powerful electromagnetic field connect with your brain and create some magic.

Just Listen.

LISTEN AND JOURNAL FROM YOUR HEART 

Listen to your heart and let it speak to you. Journal what you hear. Just let it flow. Throughout this journal you will find lined pages intended to be used for reflections from your heart.

LISTEN TO YOUR BRAIN 

Listen for new ideas and insights as your brain connects to your heart with increased cognitive abilities. You will find pages with dotted areas for brainstorming, mind-mapping, or listing new thoughts and ideas. Be open to whatever comes up and write it down.

COMMIT TO CHANGE 

When our hearts and brains join forces and send us a call to action, we are more apt to see change occur. Writing down our commitments to inspired action is a vital part of the process. Get concrete about it. Keep listening as your heart and brain work together to create strategies, timelines, and ingenious avenues for successful transformation and change. After each dotted area for journaling your ideas and insights, you will see a section with bullet points to journal specific inspired actions to create the change you want.

Throughout this journal, you will find prompt pages, based upon affirmations, with guided questions. Most of the questions have been designed with spaces for three answers. However, there are no rules or expectations. Feel free to use these pages as your heart leads you.

Just like any relationship, bringing your heart and brain into a working partnership takes time and commitment.

Rule # 1 is there are **NO RULES. Have fun** and enjoy the process of journaling at your own pace and on your own schedule as you move from heart to brain to change.

I AM *divinely* HUMAN.

DIVINE DNA FLOWS
TO ME, IN ME, AND
THROUGH ME.

I FEEL DEEP APPRECIATION FOR THESE DIVINE QUALITIES:

____

____

____

____

____

____

____

____

____

TO BRAIN

3 DIVINE QUALITIES I SEE <u>WITHIN MYSELF</u> ARE:

____

____

____

3 PEOPLE WHO I SEE DIVINE QUALITIES IN ARE:

NAME QUALITY ______________________________

NAME QUALITY ______________________________

NAME QUALITY ______________________________

3 IDEAS I HAVE ABOUT ACCESSING MORE DIVINE QUALITIES ARE:

____

____

____

TO CHANGE

3 ACTIONS I AM COMMITTED TO TAKING ARE:

____

____

____

WAYS THIS WILL TRANSFORM MY LIFE ARE:

____

____

____

MY HEART-CENTERED COMMITTMENT FOR CHANGE IS:

____

____

____

HEART

BRAIN

TO CHANGE

HEART

BRAIN

TO CHANGE

HEART ♡

BRAIN

TO CHANGE

HEART

BRAIN

TO CHANGE

HEART ♡

BRAIN

TO CHANGE

HEART

BRAIN

TO CHANGE

HEART

BRAIN

TO CHANGE

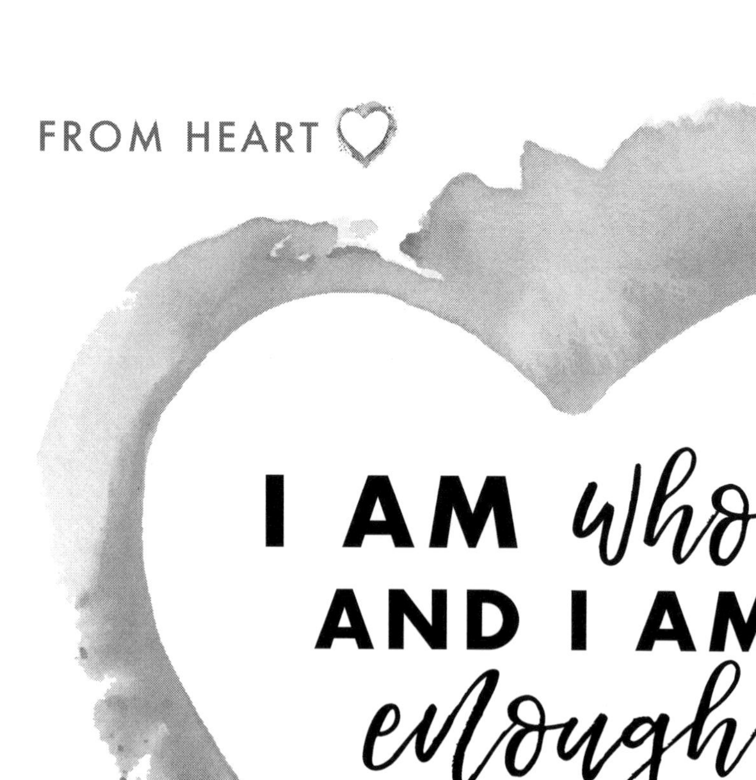

I FEEL APPRECIATION FOR MYSELF, AS I AM, IN THESE AREAS:

TO BRAIN

3 PEOPLE IN MY LIFE WHO ARE ENOUGH JUST AS THEY ARE:

____

____

____

3 AREAS IN WHICH I TEND TO JUDGE MYSELF ARE:

____

____

____

3 IDEAS I HAVE FOR INCREASING MY SELF-ACCEPTANCE ARE:

____

____

____

TO CHANGE

3 ACTIONS I AM COMMITTED TO TAKING ARE:

____

____

____

WAYS THIS WILL TRANSFORM MY LIFE ARE:

____

____

____

MY HEART-CENTERED COMMITTMENT FOR CHANGE IS:

____

____

____

HEART

BRAIN

TO CHANGE

HEART

BRAIN

TO CHANGE

HEART

BRAIN

TO CHANGE

HEART ♡

BRAIN

TO CHANGE

HEART

BRAIN

TO CHANGE

HEART ♡

BRAIN

TO CHANGE

HEART

BRAIN

TO CHANGE

PEOPLE I FEEL DEEP LOVE FOR ARE:

TO BRAIN

3 TOLERANT PEOPLE IN MY LIFE ARE:

____

____

____

3 WAYS IN WHICH I AM A LOVING PERSON ARE:

____

____

____

3 IDEAS ABOUT INCREASING LOVE AND TOLERANCE ARE:

____

____

____

TO CHANGE

3 LOVING AND TOLERANT ACTIONS I AM COMMITTED TO TAKING ARE:

____

____

____

WAYS THIS WILL TRANSFORM MY LIFE ARE:

____

____

____

MY HEART-CENTERED COMMITTMENT FOR CHANGE IS:

____

____

____

HEART ♡

BRAIN

TO CHANGE

HEART

BRAIN

TO CHANGE

HEART ♡

BRAIN

TO CHANGE

HEART

BRAIN

TO CHANGE

HEART

BRAIN

TO CHANGE

HEART ♡

BRAIN

TO CHANGE

HEART ♡

BRAIN

TO CHANGE

I AM *intuitive* AND I TRUST LIFE.

ONLY MY CREATOR HAS POWER OVER MY LIFE.

PEOPLE IN MY LIFE WHO I FEEL TRUST AND APPRECIATION FOR ARE:

TO BRAIN

3 WAYS I CAN LISTEN TO MY INTUITION ARE:

____

____

____

3 TIMES MY INTUITION GUIDED ME THAT I'M GRATEFUL FOR:

____

____

____

3 IDEAS FOR WAYS TO INCREASE MY TRUST ARE:

____

____

____

TO CHANGE

3 ACTIONS I AM COMMITTED TO TAKING ARE:

____

____

____

WAYS THIS WILL TRANSFORM MY LIFE ARE:

____

____

____

MY HEART-CENTERED COMMITTMENT FOR CHANGE IS:

____

____

____

HEART ♡

BRAIN

TO CHANGE

HEART

BRAIN

TO CHANGE

HEART ♡

BRAIN

TO CHANGE

HEART

BRAIN

TO CHANGE

HEART

BRAIN

TO CHANGE

HEART

BRAIN

TO CHANGE

HEART

BRAIN

TO CHANGE

I AM *abundant* AND I AM GENEROUS.

I OPEN MY HANDS AND HEART IN ORDER TO FREELY RELEASE AND RECEIVE.

MY HEART IS OVERFLOWING WITH APPRECIATION AND ABUNDANCE FOR:

TO BRAIN

3 WAYS THAT ABUNDANCE IS OBVIOUS IN MY LIFE ARE:

3 WAYS I WOULD LIKE TO BE MORE GENEROUS ARE:

3 IDEAS FOR WAYS I CAN CREATE GREATER ABUNDANCE AND GENEROSITY IN MY LIFE ARE:

TO CHANGE

3 ACTIONS I AM COMMITTED TO TAKING ARE:

WAYS THIS WILL TRANSFORM MY LIFE ARE:

MY HEART-CENTERED COMMITTMENT FOR CHANGE IS:

HEART

BRAIN

TO CHANGE

HEART

BRAIN

TO CHANGE

HEART ♡

BRAIN

TO CHANGE

HEART ♡

BRAIN

TO CHANGE

HEART ♡

BRAIN

TO CHANGE

HEART ♡

BRAIN

TO CHANGE

HEART

BRAIN

TO CHANGE

I AM *humble* AND I AM CONFIDENT.

I AM TRULY HUMBLED BY
THE GIFT OF LIFE AND
I BELIEVE IN MYSELF.

I AM AWESTRUCK BY THE GOODNESS OF LIFE. I AM HUMBLED BY:

____

____

____

____

____

____

____

____

____

3 AREAS THAT I FEEL CONFIDENT ABOUT MYSELF ARE:

3 AREAS WHERE I'D LIKE MORE CONFIDENCE IN MYSELF ARE:

3 IDEAS I HAVE FOR REMAINING HUMBLE YET CONFIDENT ARE:

TO CHANGE

3 ACTIONS I AM COMMITTED TO TAKING ARE:

WAYS THIS WILL TRANSFORM MY LIFE ARE:

MY HEART-CENTERED COMMITTMENT FOR CHANGE IS:

HEART ♡

BRAIN

TO CHANGE

HEART

BRAIN

TO CHANGE

HEART ♡

BRAIN

TO CHANGE

HEART ♡

BRAIN

TO CHANGE

HEART ♡

BRAIN

TO CHANGE

HEART

BRAIN

TO CHANGE

HEART

BRAIN

TO CHANGE

I AM *creative* AND I AM BEAUTIFUL.

I AM A MASTERPIECE, CREATED IN THE IMAGE OF THE CREATOR OF ALL BEAUTY.

BEAUTIFUL ASPECTS OF MYSELF THAT I FEEL APPRECIATION FOR:

TO BRAIN

3 NEW WAYS THAT I CAN DEFINE BEAUTY ARE:

____

____

____

3 THINGS I HAVE CREATED IN MY LIFE ARE:

____

____

____

3 IDEAS FOR CREATING MORE BEAUTY IN THE WORLD ARE:

____

____

____

TO CHANGE

3 BEAUTIFUL OR CREATIVE ACTIONS I AM COMMITTED TO TAKING ARE:

____

____

____

WAYS THAT SEEING MYSELF AS BEAUTIFUL OR CREATIVE WILL TRANSFORM MY LIFE ARE:

____

____

____

MY HEART-CENTERED COMMITTMENT FOR CHANGE IS:

____

____

____

HEART

BRAIN

TO CHANGE

HEART

BRAIN

TO CHANGE

HEART ♡

BRAIN

TO CHANGE

HEART

BRAIN

TO CHANGE

HEART ♡

BRAIN

TO CHANGE

HEART ♡

BRAIN

TO CHANGE

HEART ♡

BRAIN

TO CHANGE

I AM *bold* AND I AM RESILIENT.

RESILIENT AND/OR BOLD PEOPLE I FEEL APPRECIATION FOR ARE:

TO BRAIN

3 TIMES WHEN I HAVE SHOWN BOLDNESS ARE:

____

____

____

3 TIMES WHEN I HAVE BOUNCED BACK FROM ADVERSITY ARE:

____

____

____

3 IDEAS TO INCREASE MY BOLDNESS/RESILIENCE ARE:

____

____

____

TO CHANGE

3 BOLD ACTIONS I AM COMMITTED TO TAKING ARE:

____

____

____

WAYS THIS WILL TRANSFORM MY LIFE ARE:

____

____

____

MY HEART-CENTERED COMMITTMENT FOR CHANGE IS:

____

____

____

HEART ♡

BRAIN

TO CHANGE

HEART

BRAIN

TO CHANGE

HEART

BRAIN

TO CHANGE

HEART ♡

BRAIN

TO CHANGE

HEART

BRAIN

TO CHANGE

HEART

BRAIN

TO CHANGE

HEART ♡

BRAIN

TO CHANGE

I AM *healthy* AND I AM WELL.

MY BODY CONTAINS WISDOM FOR BALANCE AND PERFECT HEALTH.

THINGS ABOUT MY HEALTH THAT I FEEL GRATEFUL FOR ARE:

TO BRAIN

3 SPECIFIC TIMES MY BODY HAS HEALED ITSELF ARE:

____

____

____

3 WAYS I DEFINE WELLBEING ARE:

____

____

____

3 IDEAS FOR TAKING GREATER RESPONSIBILITY FOR MY OWN HEALTH AND WELLBEING ARE:

____

____

____

TO CHANGE

3 ACTIONS I AM COMMITTED TO TAKING ARE:

____

____

____

WAYS THIS WILL TRANSFORM MY LIFE ARE:

____

____

____

MY HEART-CENTERED COMMITTMENT FOR CHANGE IS:

____

____

____

HEART ♡

BRAIN

TO CHANGE

HEART

BRAIN

TO CHANGE

HEART

BRAIN

TO CHANGE

HEART ♡

BRAIN

TO CHANGE

HEART ♡

BRAIN

TO CHANGE

HEART ♡

BRAIN

TO CHANGE

HEART

BRAIN

TO CHANGE

I AM *empathetic* AND I AM FORGIVING.

I FEEL DEEP GRATITUDE FOR THE EMPATHY AND/OR FORGIVENESS I HAVE RECEIVED FROM:

TO BRAIN

3 TIMES THAT I HAVE SHOWN EMPATHY AND/OR FORGIVENESS ARE:

____

____

____

3 TIMES OTHERS HAVE SHOWN EMPATHY AND/OR FORGIVENESS TO ME ARE:

____

____

____

3 IDEAS FOR IMPLEMENTING GREATER EMPATHY AND FORGIVENESS ARE:

____

____

____

TO CHANGE

3 ACTIONS I AM COMMITTED TO TAKING ARE:

____

____

____

WAYS THIS WILL TRANSFORM MY LIFE ARE:

____

____

____

MY HEART-CENTERED COMMITTMENT FOR CHANGE IS:

____

____

____

HEART

BRAIN

TO CHANGE

HEART ♡

BRAIN

TO CHANGE

HEART

BRAIN

TO CHANGE

HEART ♡

BRAIN

TO CHANGE

HEART ♡

BRAIN

TO CHANGE

HEART ♡

BRAIN

TO CHANGE

HEART ♡

BRAIN

TO CHANGE

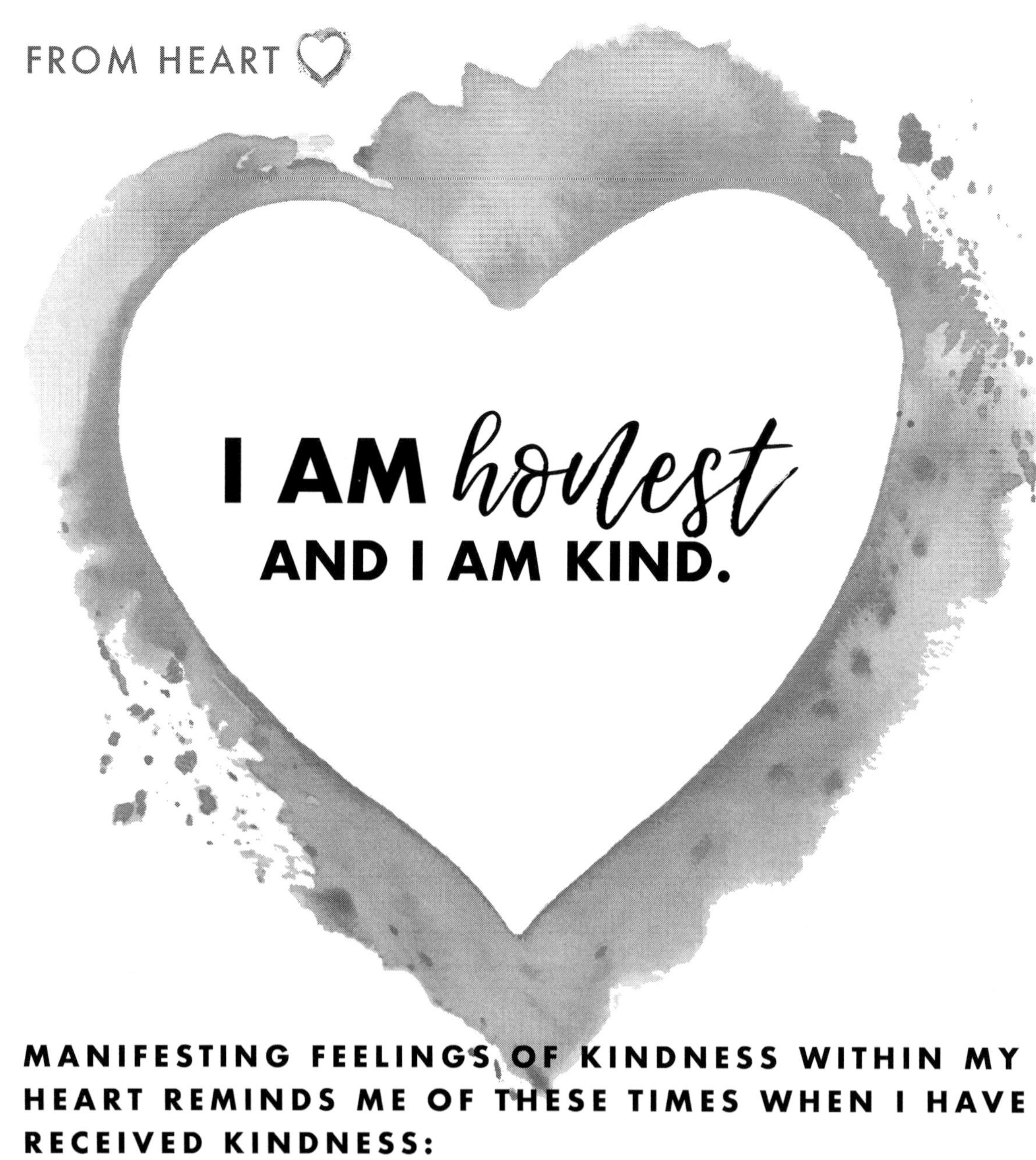

MANIFESTING FEELINGS OF KINDNESS WITHIN MY HEART REMINDS ME OF THESE TIMES WHEN I HAVE RECEIVED KINDNESS:

TO BRAIN

3 WAYS THAT BEING HONEST IS KIND ARE:

____

____

____

3 AREAS WHERE I CAN BE MORE HONEST ARE:

____

____

____

3 IDEAS I HAVE ABOUT TRUE KINDNESS AND HONESTY ARE:

____

____

____

TO CHANGE

3 KIND OR HONEST ACTIONS I AM COMMITTED TO TAKING ARE:

____

____

____

WAYS THIS WILL TRANSFORM MY LIFE ARE:

____

____

____

MY HEART-CENTERED COMMITTMENT FOR CHANGE IS:

____

____

____

HEART ♡

BRAIN

TO CHANGE

HEART ♡

BRAIN

TO CHANGE

HEART ♡

BRAIN

TO CHANGE

HEART

BRAIN

TO CHANGE

HEART ♡

BRAIN

TO CHANGE

HEART ♡

BRAIN

TO CHANGE

HEART ♡

BRAIN

TO CHANGE

I AM *expansive* AND I AM APPRECIATIVE.

AS I FILL MY HEART WITH APPRECIATION, I FEEL MY HEART EXPANDING AND SENDING LOVE TO:

TO BRAIN

3 THINGS I AM FILLED WITH APPRECIATION FOR ARE:

___

___

___

3 AREAS THAT I AM AWARE I HAVE RESTRICTED MY HEART IN ARE:

___

___

___

3 IDEAS I HAVE FOR EXPANSION ARE:

___

___

___

TO CHANGE

3 ACTIONS I AM COMMITTED TO TAKING ARE:

___

___

___

WAYS THIS WILL TRANSFORM MY LIFE ARE:

___

___

___

MY HEART-CENTERED COMMITTMENT FOR CHANGE IS:

___

___

___

HEART

BRAIN

TO CHANGE

HEART ♡

BRAIN

TO CHANGE

HEART

BRAIN

TO CHANGE

HEART ♡

BRAIN

TO CHANGE

HEART

BRAIN

TO CHANGE

HEART

BRAIN

TO CHANGE

HEART

BRAIN

TO CHANGE

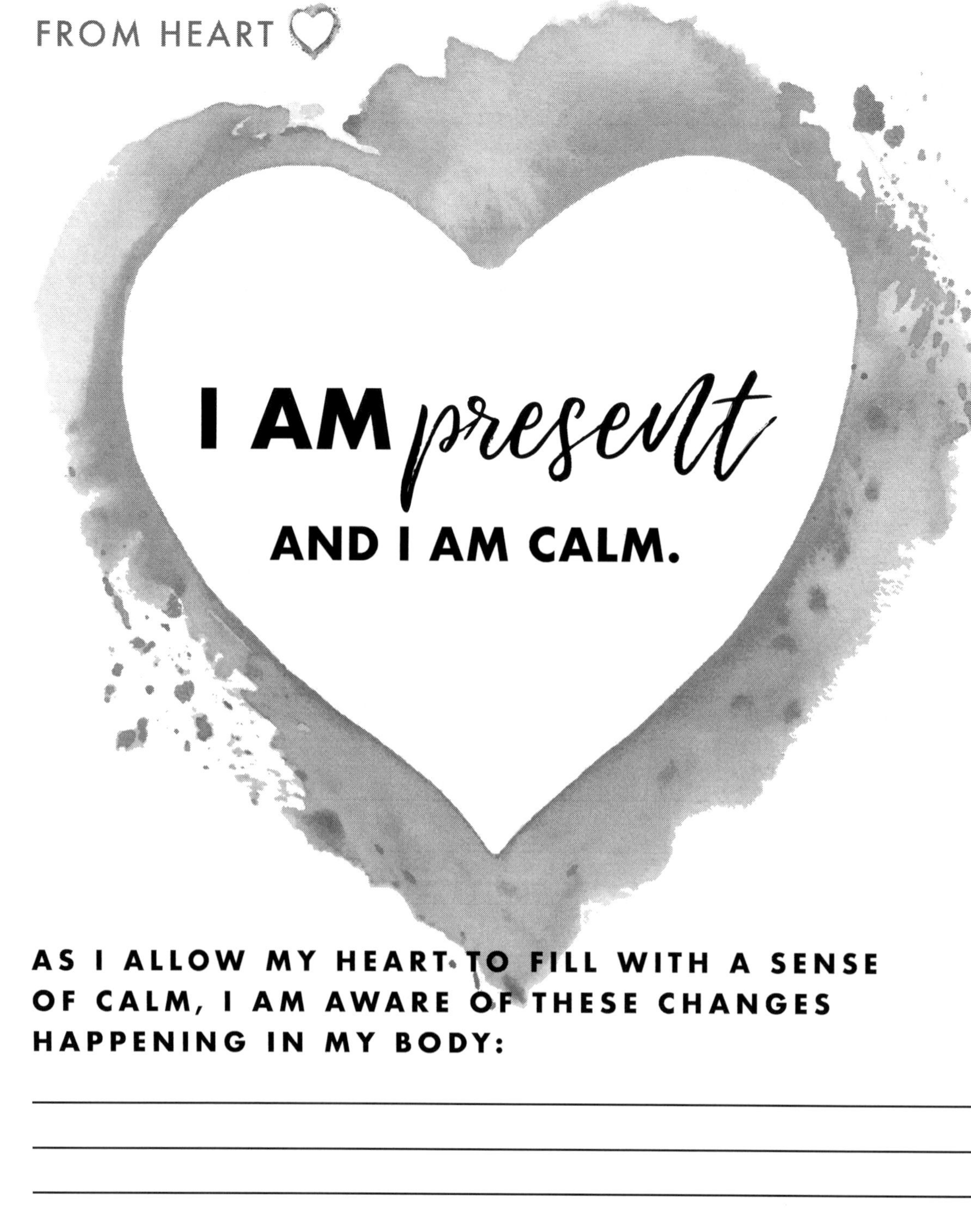

AS I ALLOW MY HEART TO FILL WITH A SENSE OF CALM, I AM AWARE OF THESE CHANGES HAPPENING IN MY BODY:

TO BRAIN

3 NEW THINGS I BECOME AWARE OF WHEN FOCUSING ON THIS PRESENT MOMENT ARE:

____

____

____

3 POSSIBLE WAYS BEING MORE CALM AND PRESENT CAN AFFECT MY HEALTH ARE:

____

____

____

3 IDEAS TO BE MORE PRESENT AND CALM ARE:

____

____

____

TO CHANGE

3 ACTIONS I AM COMMITTED TO TAKING ARE:

____

____

____

WAYS THIS WILL TRANSFORM MY LIFE ARE:

____

____

____

MY HEART-CENTERED COMMITTMENT FOR CHANGE IS:

____

____

____

HEART ♡

BRAIN

TO CHANGE

HEART

BRAIN

TO CHANGE

HEART

BRAIN

TO CHANGE

HEART ♡

BRAIN

TO CHANGE

HEART ♡

BRAIN

TO CHANGE

HEART

BRAIN

TO CHANGE

HEART

BRAIN

TO CHANGE

I AM *purposeful* AND I AM EMPOWERED.

I AM THE HERO I'VE BEEN WAITING FOR.

AS I IMAGINE MY BREATH CARRYING POWER AND PURPOSE INTO MY HEART, I AM AWARE OF:

TO BRAIN

3 LIMITING "BELIEFS" I AM AWARE OF HAVING ARE:

____

____

____

3 TIMES I HAVE FELT POWERFUL AND ON "PURPOSE" ARE:

____

____

____

3 IDEAS I HAVE ABOUT MY PURPOSE ARE:

____

____

____

TO CHANGE

3 PURPOSEFUL AND EMPOWERED ACTIONS I AM COMMITTED TO TAKING ARE:

____

____

____

WAYS THIS WILL TRANSFORM MY LIFE ARE:

____

____

____

MY HEART-CENTERED COMMITTMENT FOR CHANGE IS:

____

____

____

HEART ♡

BRAIN

TO CHANGE

HEART ♡

BRAIN
TO CHANGE

HEART ♡

BRAIN

TO CHANGE

HEART

BRAIN

TO CHANGE

HEART ♡

BRAIN

TO CHANGE

HEART ♡

BRAIN

TO CHANGE

HEART ♡

BRAIN

TO CHANGE

HEART-CENTERED REFLECTIONS AND REVELATIONS

FROM THE HEART

Reflections looking back

THINGS MY HEART HAS TAUGHT ME:

Revelations for moving forward

WHAT IS MY HEART TELLING ME NOW?

Reflections looking back

HEART-CENTERED INSIGHTS AND IDEAS I HAVE IMPLEMENTED SO FAR:

Revelations for moving forward

HEART-CENTERED IDEAS FOR MOVING FORWARD:

Reflections on transformation

ACTIONS I HAVE TAKEN:

WAYS HEART-CENTERED ACTIONS HAVE CHANGED MY LIFE:

Revelations for continuing my transformation

MY HEART-CENTERED COMMITTMENT FOR ONGOING ACTION AND CHANGE IS:

ABOUT PEGGY

Peggy Johnson has been a certified Life Coach with a BA in Counseling/Psychology since 2009 but has been working in the field of Human Development for over 30 years. She sees the best in people and nothing brings her greater joy than seeing someone's heart light up with the realization of how truly amazing and capable they are. With additional certifications as a Canfield Success Principles trainer, and through the HeartMath Institute*, Peggy's heart-centered, action oriented approach brings a unique blend of science, spirituality, and practical strategies for change into her business as well as her personal life.

For more information on products or services provided by Peggy please email her at info@peggycares.com, or visit her website at www.hopeactualized.com.

VISIT PEGGY'S SHOP!

**HeartMath is a registered trademark of Quantum Intech, Inc.*

Made in the USA
Columbia, SC
10 February 2020

87655258R00130